636.8083
E24c

101 ESSENTIAL TIPS

CAT CARE

ESSENTIAL **101** TIPS

CAT CARE

Andrew Edney, David Taylor

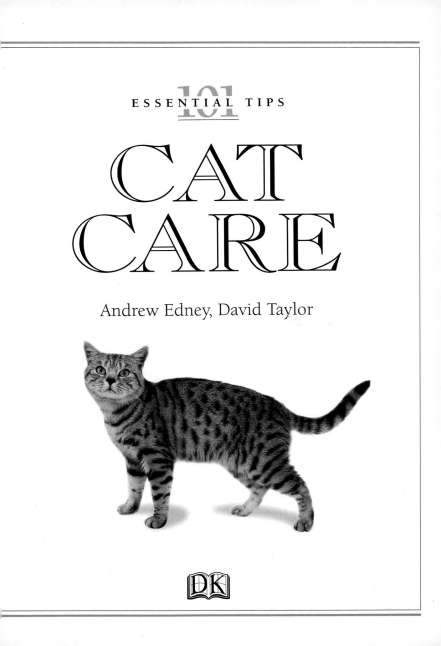

DK

LONDON, NEW YORK, MELBOURNE,
MUNICH AND DELHI

Editor Susie Behar
Art Editor Colin Walton
Managing Editor Gillian Roberts
Managing Art Editor Karen Sawyer
Category Publisher Mary-Clare Jerram
DTP Designer Sonia Charbonnier
Production Controller Luca Frassinetti

First American edition, 1995
This paperback edition published in the United States in 2003
by DK Publishing, Inc.
375 Hudson Street, New York, New York 10014
Penguin Group (US)

A Cataloging-in-Publication record for this book is available from the Library of Congress

ISBN 0–7894–9689–5

Color reproduced in Singapore by Bright Arts
Printed in Hong Kong by Wing King Tong

See our complete product line at
www.dk.com

ESSENTIAL TIPS 101

HOW TO CHOOSE A CAT

1 WHY BUY A CAT?

A cat is a wonderful pet. It is entertaining, affectionate, and astoundingly self-reliant, although, like any pet, it requires proper care. Since a cat can live indoors and does not need to be taken for a daily walk, it is the ideal pet for a city-dweller. Cats make particularly good pets for children or the elderly.

GOOD COMPANY
Stroking a pet helps to relieve stress and lower blood pressure.

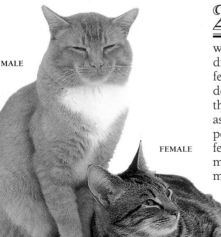

MALE

FEMALE

2 WHICH SEX?

Before making your choice, weigh the advantages and disadvantages of owning a male or female cat. The female cat is more docile, playful, and affectionate than the male. The larger and more assertive male will stray and fight for possession of territory and the females within it. If, however, your male cat is neutered, it will become more docile and "female-like."

MALE VERSUS FEMALE
Once neutered, there are few behavioral differences between a male and female cat.

3 KITTEN OR ADULT?

A kitten is more demanding to look after than an adult cat. Playful and inquisitive, it will need careful watching, as well as litter and cat-door training. But a kitten is more adaptable than an adult cat and easier to introduce into your home, especially if you already have a pet. Also, a kitten, well-trained from an early age, will be less trouble to look after as it grows up than an older cat with ingrained habits.

△ PLAYMATE
Give a kitten plenty of toys to keep it occupied and, ideally, a playmate if you are often out during the day.

◁ MOTHERLY LOVE
If you decide to buy a kitten, do not take it away from its mother until it is fully weaned, usually at eight weeks old.

△ OLDER CAT
Consider an older cat if you don't want to rear a kitten. Older cats can be obtained from animal welfare shelters.

4 WHY A SHORTHAIR?

A shorthaired cat will make fewer demands on your time than a longhaired cat; it is able to groom itself, so you will expend far less energy keeping its coat in good condition. Also, many of the coat problems that arise on a longhair, such as matted hair, are less likely to occur, and it is easier to tend to wounds and remove parasites.

△ SELF-GROOMING
You need to groom a shorthair once a week since it will manage the job well on its own.

ATTENTION-SEEKERS ▷
A famous shorthaired breed is the Siamese. Known to be very vocal and demanding of human attention, they are considered "doglike" in their devotion.

Typical shorthaired coat

ON THE PROWL
Generally, shorthaired cats are more active and independent than longhairs, so if you lead a busy life a shorthair is probably preferable.

5 WHY A LONGHAIR?

Luxuriant tail fur

Dense longhair coat

The spectacular coat of a longhair is its main asset. It requires daily brushing and untangling. If you do not groom your longhair daily, clumps of swallowed hair, known as hairballs, accumulate in its stomach, upsetting its digestion. However, the look and docile nature compensate for the grooming demands.

DAILY TASK
Longhairs require daily grooming. Neglected coats soon look disheveled and may become matted.

SEMILONGHAIRS ▷
If you like the longhair's appearance, but don't have time to groom daily, consider a semi-longhair, which has a long top coat but a much thinner undercoat.

△ **FLOPPY RAGDOLL**
The Ragdoll is particularly docile. Whenever picked up, it relaxes its muscles and flops into the carrier's arms, hence its name.

Semi-longhair coat

6 WHY A PEDIGREE?

Buy a pedigree if you aim to show or breed it. If you intend to show your pedigree, make this clear when you buy a kitten. Some pedigree kittens are not up to show standard, and the breeder will be able to identify potential winners. Since each pedigree breed has its own physical and behavioral characteristics, if you opt for a pedigree, you will have a good idea of how your kitten will look and behave as an adult cat. A major disadvantage, however, is the expense.

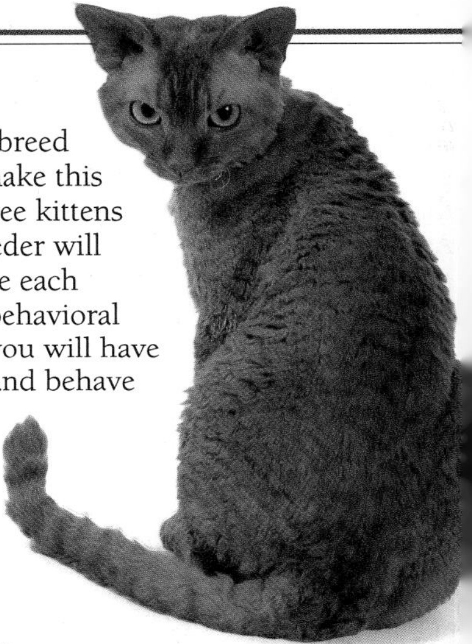

FAMILY LIKENESS ▽
Controlled pedigree breeding ensures that looks are passed from generation to generation.

Strong familial likeness

△ DEVON REX
There are over 100 pedigree breeds. Some, like the Devon Rex, are relatively new breeds.

Well-groomed coat

PRIZEWINNER ▷
A show cat requires a significant investment of time and money but, for many people, the thrill of competing overrides such concerns.

7 WHY A NONPEDIGREE?

If all you want is a feline friend or family pet, choose a nonpedigree: as companions, they are no less superior than pedigree cats. An enormous variety of nonpedigree cats is available, although the majority have some type of tabby marking and coloring. The main advantage is that they are much less expensive to buy – indeed you can often obtain them free.

Long, glossy coat

◁ **LESS WORRY**
Owning a nonpedigree is far less worrying as owning a valuable, and usually less hardy, pedigree cat.

△ **JUST AS PRETTY**
Many nonpedigrees are as attractive as pedigrees and far less expensive.

Shorthair coat

THE TABBY
Since the gene for tabby markings is dominant, most nonpedigrees are tabbies, and are usually friendly to humans.

Variable markings

13

8 WHERE TO BUY A CAT

If you are looking for a pedigree cat, go to a specialist breeder. Animal welfare societies are a good source of abandoned and lost cats or cats whose original owners have died. Alternatively, your vet may know of cats that need a good home.

△ FROM A SHELTER
Give an unwanted cat a home and a happy life by obtaining your new pet from a shelter.

◁ FROM A PET STORE
Cats can be bought from pet stores, although it is wise to get a veterinary health check before you make a purchase.

9 CHECKUP & VACCINATION

As soon as you buy a kitten, register it with a vet. The best way to choose a vet is to ask your cat-owning neighbors to recommend one. It is essential to have your cat vaccinated against two potentially fatal viruses, Feline Enteritis and Feline Influenza, usually at nine weeks old. If you are buying an adult cat, check that it was vaccinated as a kitten, has since received regular boosters, and has an up-to-date certificate.

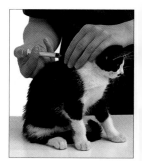

NEW KITTEN CHECKUP ▷
The vet will give your kitten a health check and provide you with a written health certificate. The vet may also ask questions about your cat's behavior; unusual behavior in cats is often a symptom of illness.

△ VACCINATION & BOOSTER
Although vaccinations are not dangerous, they should be given to healthy kittens: they are not wholly effective in unhealthy cats. After the initial shots, your cat will need further vaccinations three to four weeks later.

10 PEDIGREE REGISTRATION

Register your pedigree kitten with the appropriate cat authority. This is especially important if you intend to show it. Your vet can advise you on the procedure. If your cat is already registered, notify the authority of change of ownership.

- Registration usually takes place when a kitten is five weeks old.
- Register the cat's name, details of coloring, and parentage.
- If you buy a cat that is already registered, make sure that you are given the documentation.

11 NEUTERING

Unless you aim to breed your cat, you should have it neutered. This prevents pregnancy in females and undesirable sexual behavior in males. If a female cat is not neutered, she will come into heat several times a year, during which time she may mate. A full tom will stray, spray urine, and fight with other males. The operation is performed under anesthetic and takes only a few days to heal.

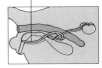

MALE

FEMALE

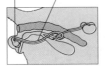

Uterus
Vagina / Ovaries   Vagina

Testes   Spermatic cord   Spermatic cord

SPAYING (FEMALE NEUTERING)
A female should be spayed at four or five months old and never during estrus (heat). The operation removes the ovaries and the uterus and leaves a small skin wound. She may be kept overnight at the vet's.

CASTRATING (MALE NEUTERING)
A male should be castrated at six months. The male's testes are removed. There are normally no stitches and the cat will heal quickly. A male should not be neutered before its penis is fully developed.

12 EXAMINE YOUR KITTEN

Think twice before you choose that adorable, helpless-looking kitten. Since a cat's lifespan can be 15 years, buying a healthy kitten may save you many years of veterinary fees.

▽ **WHICH KITTEN?**
At first sight all kittens in a litter look similar. On closer inspection, however, you will be able to tell which is lively, which is shy, and which is timid. Watch them play to check for vitality or lameness.

Curious kitten

Attentive kitten

Alert kitten

Sleepy kitten

HOW TO SEX A KITTEN ▷
Determining the sex of a kitten can be surprisingly difficult. Lift up the kitten's tail and study the opening beneath the anus. A female's vulva is situated close to the anus, while the male has a larger gap between the anus, testes (raised dark area), and penis.

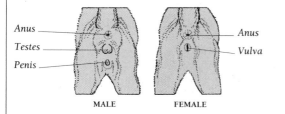

Anus
Testes
Penis

Anus
Vulva

MALE   FEMALE

1 The rear should be clean. Lift the tail gently and check for any signs of diarrhea (*see p.56*) or discharge.

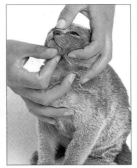

2 The kitten's ears should be clean and dry. If there is any dark-colored wax or if the kitten is scratching, it may have ear mites (see p.54). Never poke anything into the delicate ear canal.

3 Bright eyes, free from discharge, are a sign of a healthy kitten. Check that the third eyelid isn't showing (see p.53).

4 The nose should feel velvety and slightly moist, and the nostrils should be free of any discharge. Listen to the kitten's breathing. If it is unsteady, the kitten may have a viral infection.

5 Pry open the kitten's mouth. A healthy cat will have pale pink, uninflamed gums, white teeth, and odor-free breath.

6 The abdomen should be rounded but not pot-bellied. When picked up, the kitten should feel a little heavier than it looks.

7 The coat should be smooth, soft, and glossy. Part the coat to check for evidence of parasites or flea dirt.

HOUSING & HANDLING

13 BASIC EQUIPMENT

Be prepared for your new cat's needs by having the essential cat-care equipment ready. A wide variety of products, at a range of prices, is available. Shop around to make a good choice.

SHOVEL

LITTER BOX

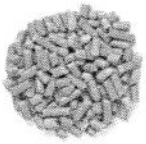

FORK

SPOON

WATER BOWL

△ **FEEDING**
Put aside a fork, spoon, water bowl, and food bowl. Keep the equipment clean with dish detergent. Avoid disinfectants; some are not safe for cats.

FOOD BOWL

WOOD PELLETS

△ **CLEANING**
To keep your home hygienic, a litter box and supply of litter are essential.

BRUSH    COMB

△ **GROOMING**
For good grooming, buy a selection of brushes and combs (see pp.36–43).

CAT TOYS

△ **PLAY TIME**
Buy a selection of toys to help keep your kitten occupied.

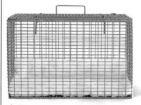

△ **TRAVEL**
A cat carrier is essential for transporting a cat safely.

△ **BEDDING**
Buy a comfortable bed to help your cat sleep well.

14 HOW TO LIFT A CAT

Approach a cat cautiously. Do not grab it; ideally, let it approach you. Begin your contact with gentle stroking. When the cat is used to your touch, pick it up.

1 Hold the cat with one hand under its chest and the other under its hindquarters. Let the sternum rest in the hand.

2 ▷ Lift the cat gently, drawing it toward your chest. Give full support to its hindquarters.

15 HOW TO HOLD A CAT

Most cats enjoy being picked up and held, although only on their terms. Usually, a cat does not like being held for more than a short time. If you stroke a cat while you hold it, it will be reassured. Once it starts to struggle, let it down. If you hold a cat against its will, it may bite or scratch you.

CRADLE A KITTEN
Hold a kitten gently, supporting its whole body.

IN YOUR ARMS
Rest the cat's paws in the crook of your arm.

ON YOUR SHOULDER
Put the paws on a shoulder, supporting the hindquarters.

16 LITTER TRAINING

Place the litter box in a quiet corner. When the kitten looks as if it is ready to use it – it will crouch with its tail raised – place it in the litter box. A natural instinct will tell the kitten to cover up its feces with the litter. If a kitten relieves itself outside the box, never rub its nose in the mess – the odor will tell the kitten that this is its toilet area and it will return to it.

EARLY LEARNERS
You can teach a kitten as young as four weeks old to use a litter box.

17 LITTER BOXES & LITTER

Two types of litter box are available: covered and open. The advantage of a covered box is that if your kitten is shy it will be more inclined to use a private area. If the kitten doesn't use the litter box it may be that the litter odor is offensive; luckily, however, there is a variety of litters available. Before filling the box with litter, line it with newspaper or litter-box liners.

Open box

Scoop

COVERED BOX   **LINERS**   **PAPER**

REUSABLE LITTER
A washable, non-absorbent litter.

FULLER'S EARTH
A litter based on natural clay.

LIGHTWEIGHT
A convenient litter to carry.

FIBER-BASED
A litter that absorbs liquid well.

18 INTRODUCTION TO OTHER PETS

When you introduce a new kitten to the other pets in your household, feed them separately for the first few weeks and supervise their meetings. The most difficult introduction is that of a kitten to an older cat, which may feel threatened.

SAFE HAVEN ▷
When you first bring your kitten home, make sure it has an area of its own where it can feel safe. Let the kitten acclimatize.

CAT MEETS DOG ▷
Take control of the first meetings by keeping the dog on a leash, or by placing the cat in a small play pen. Once dog and cat are used to each other, they can safely be left alone.

◁ CAT MEETS CAT
Allow the cat to sniff the kitten and, if the cat should attack, separate them immediately. It may take as long as a month for them to settle down.

CAT MEETS RABBIT ▷
Supervise a kitten in the company of rabbits or guinea pigs: if a kitten climbs over a small animal, even in play, it may harm it. Do not let a small animal out of its cage if an adult cat is around.

19 ESTABLISH ROUTINES

You cannot train a cat in the same way that you can train a dog but, by establishing routines, you will make life easier for yourself and more enjoyable for your cat. It is important for your cat to recognize its name; by calling it at feeding and bedtime, it will soon learn to respond.

△ GROOMING
Groom a longhair at the same time each day – after feeding is a good time. Groom a shorthair once a week at a regular time.

◁ FEEDING
Feed your cat regularly in the same place and at the same time every day.

◁ PLAYING
Playtime is essential to a cat's development, especially if your cat is an indoor cat. Spend 10–15 minutes a day playing with your cat.

△ SLEEPING
Place the bed in a quiet spot. At first your cat may try to sleep on your bed. If you don't want to encourage this, place the cat in its own bed and keep it in its "bedroom" for the night.

20 KEEP AN INDOOR CAT HAPPY

Cats, unlike some dogs, can live indoors quite contentedly, especially if they have never known any other life. If you keep your cat inside, make sure it has plenty of toys for amusement and exercise. Alternatively, buy two kittens at the same time, so that they can play with each other.

◁ **CREATURE COMFORT**
Cats sleep up to 16 hours a day, so if you give your cat a comfortable bed, it is likely to stay out of mischief.

△ **HOME WRECKERS**
If you don't provide your kitten with toys, it will become bored and restless and may start to destroy your possessions.

21 GOOD SCRATCHING

To prevent your cat ruining your furniture by scratching it, provide it with a scratching post. When your cat starts scratching, place its paws on the post.

MANMADE POST ▷
A post impregnated with catnip and hung with toys makes a good scratching post.

◁ **THE REAL THING**
If your cat is allowed outdoors, it will probably find a piece of bark on which to sharpen its claws.

22 COMMON INDOOR HAZARDS

Curiosity really can kill the cat, so closing doors, windows, boxes, and lids is a necessary precaution to keep a cat from potential hazards such as open washing machines and garbage cans. Breakable objects, poisonous plants (*see p.67*), and food should be kept out of your cat's reach.

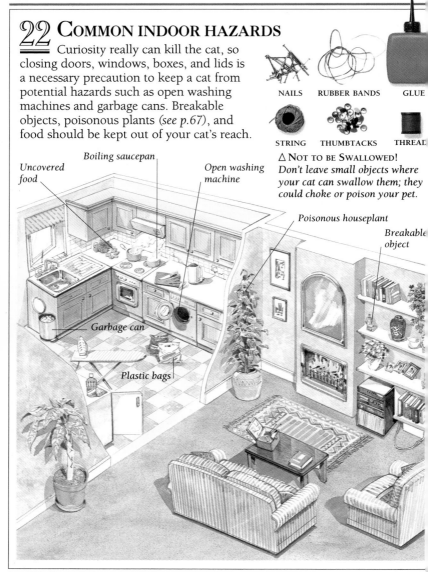

NAILS **RUBBER BANDS** **GLUE**

STRING **THUMBTACKS** **THREAD**

△ **NOT TO BE SWALLOWED!**
Don't leave small objects where your cat can swallow them; they could choke or poison your pet.

Boiling saucepan

Uncovered food

Open washing machine

Poisonous houseplant

Breakable object

Garbage can

Plastic bags

23 AN INDOOR LAWN

Grass is a good source of fiber for your cat. It also acts as a useful emetic, which will help your cat to regurgitate unwanted matter such as hairballs. If you keep your pet permanently indoors, provide it with some greenery to chew. This could be grass, catnip, thyme, sage, or parsley.

INDOOR GREENERY

24 ALLOWING A NEW CAT OUTDOORS

Most cats want to explore the outside environment as soon as possible, so, for the first few weeks, you will probably have to restrain your cat from rushing outside every time you open the door. Once your cat is familiar with its new home, you can let it out under supervision.

KEEP WATCH ▽
Supervise your cat's first trip outside.

△ **THE URGE TO BE OUTDOORS**
Keep your cat inside until you are sure that outdoor conditions are suitable (see below).

DO'S & DON'TS
- *Do not let your cat out in bad weather.*
- *Whenever you let your cat out, make sure it wears a collar.*
- *Do not let your cat outside until it has been vaccinated.*

25 CAT DOOR TRAINING

When you are satisfied that your cat is ready to go outdoors on its own, you should mount a cat door. A cat door will give your cat the freedom to come and go as it pleases. It is important that you mount the door at the right height for the cat to step through: about 6 in (15 cm) from the floor. Most cats learn how to use the door quickly.

1 If at first your cat does not want to approach the cat door, place your cat near the door and prop open the door.

2 To encourage the cat through the door, tempt it with food placed on the outside, or gently lift the cat through.

3 It should not take long for your cat to learn to push the door open. If your cat has difficulty passing through the door, it could be that the door is too high off the floor.

26 CAT DOOR CHOICE

Cat doors are available in varying degrees of sophistication. Some open inward and outward, others only inward, so the cat can enter but not leave the house, and some have a locking device, which is useful if you want to prevent your cat from going out at night. The most expensive are electromagnetic doors, which can only be opened by a magnet worn on the cat's collar.

LOCKABLE DOOR
Prevent your cat from going out at night by installing a lockable door.

STANDARD DOOR
This basic door has no locking device to prevent stray cats from visiting you.

27 COMMON OUTDOOR HAZARDS

If you live on a busy road and don't have a yard, it is probably not safe to let your cat go outside. Even if you have a yard, there are still some potential hazards. Sharp garden tools and pesticides must be kept out of your cat's reach. You should also check that you do not have any poisonous garden plants (*see p.67*).

SHEARS

PESTICIDES   PLANT FERTILIZERS

△ **TOOLS & POISONS**
Keep tools, pesticides, and fertilizers in a catproof shed, and ensure you don't leave them lying around outside.

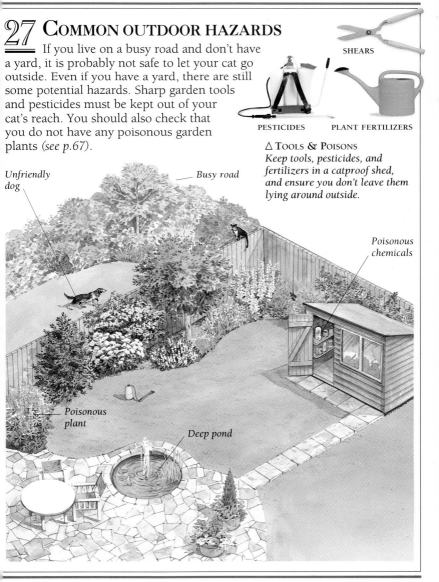

Unfriendly dog

Busy road

Poisonous chemicals

Poisonous plant

Deep pond

27

28 CHOOSING A COLLAR

A cat that is allowed outside should always wear a collar and name tag. Whichever type of collar you select, make sure it fits properly and that it has an elasticated safety section.

PLAIN COLLAR

REFLECTIVE COLLAR

NATURAL FLEA COLLAR

IDENTITY DISK **IDENTITY BARREL** **BELL**

NAME & ADDRESS
An identity disk or barrel with your cat's name and address should be worn on the collar at all times.

TEST FOR TIGHTNESS
Make sure that the collar fits well. If it is too tight it may irritate the neck skin; if it is too loose, the cat may learn how to slip it off.

29 HOW TO WALK A CAT

It is possible to take a cat for a walk on a leash. First, train the cat to wear a harness, then attach a leash, and let the cat become used to trailing the leash. Once it is accustomed to this, try walking it in the house or yard. In time, take it for a walk in a park. If your cat resists, do not force it to walk.

ORIENTAL

BURMESE

SIAMESE **RUSSIAN BLUE**

△ **SOME CATS YOU CAN WALK**
Oriental cats are known as the easiest cats to train to walk on a leash.

TAKE YOUR CAT FOR A STROLL

30 THE TRAVELING CAT

Cats are not very good travelers, so if your cat has to go on a journey, place it in a suitable carrier. Cat carriers are made from wicker, wire, plastic, and cardboard. The carrier should be strong and well ventilated. Never let a cat roam free on the back seat of a car or leave a cat alone in a car on a warm day – if you must leave a cat unattended, make sure there is ventilation and keep it out of direct sunlight. If the journey lasts for more than half an hour, stop to let the cat use a litter box and to eat and drink.

SAFE JOURNEY
Traveling cats should be confined in a proper cat carrier.

1 Place the cat carrier in an enclosed space, so that if your cat struggles free, you will be able to catch it quickly.

2 When the cat is inside the carrier, check that the door is securely fastened, and then take it to the car.

31 WHEN YOU MOVE

Cats have a strong homing instinct, so when you move, help your cat acclimatize to its new surroundings. Do not place your cat in the moving van, but take it with you in your car. On arrival, provide it with food, water, and a litter box, and do not let it outside for about five days. If your cat turns up missing soon after moving, look for it at your previous home. It is not unusual for a cat to return to its old hunting ground.

BACK-SEAT PASSENGER

32 TRANSPORT A CAT

If your cat is traveling by air, road, rail, or sea, place it in a container approved by the carrying company. You will find specially designed containers available in pet stores. The container should be strong, light, and well ventilated. Mark instructions for feeding and watering and the owner's name and address clearly on the carrier.

- Check the carrying company's regulations in advance of your trip.
- Female cats suckling their young and unweaned cats are not accepted for carriage by most airlines.
- In aircraft containers, cats and dogs are kept apart, unless they come from the same household.
- Check international and national travel requirements before you travel.

Adequate ventilation is vital

A handle for carrying is essential

SPECIALLY-BUILT
A specially designed, rigid container is the best way to transport a cat.

Containers must be wel constructed so that the cat cannot be harmed

33 QUARANTINE

Rabies is a potentially fatal virus for both animals and humans. It is spread through the saliva of an infected animal. Most rabies-free countries enforce strict measures to prevent the spread of the virus. Anyone who violates a country's quarantine regulations, and smuggles an animal into a protected country, may face severe penalties.

- A cat taken abroad may have to spend a period of time in quarantine either on its arrival or return home.
- In the US, if you are traveling between states with an animal, you must have the required vaccination and health documents.
- Different countries have different quarantine rules. Your vet will be able to give you helpful information.

34 CATTERY CHOICE

If you are going away for a few days, ask a neighbor to drop into your home once a day to feed your cat. If this is not feasible, move it into a cattery. Check out the cattery before you reserve it. It should be clean, secure, and, although the cats should be able to see each other, they should not be able to make physical contact. Don't forget to give the cattery any necessary dietary instructions.

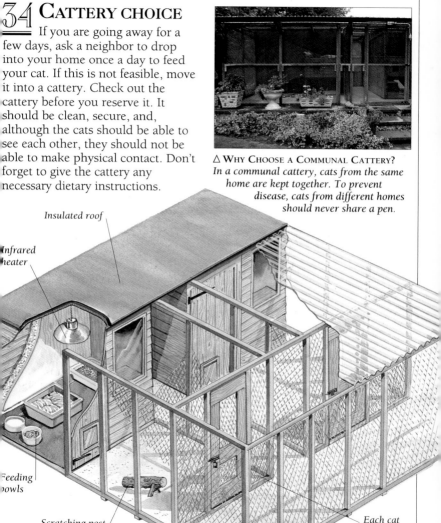

△ **WHY CHOOSE A COMMUNAL CATTERY?**
In a communal cattery, cats from the same home are kept together. To prevent disease, cats from different homes should never share a pen.

Insulated roof

Infrared heater

Feeding bowls

Scratching post

Each cat has its own pen

FEEDING TIPS

35 ESSENTIAL EQUIPMENT

Since cats are fussy eaters, provide them with wholesome food, and clean food and water bowls. Keep your cat-feeding equipment separate from your own – storing it in a plastic container is a good idea. If you are going away, use an automatic feeder. This is a closed feeding bowl fitted with a timing device that opens at preset times.

- Don't serve food in a dirty bowl; the cat won't eat it.
- Don't use an automatic feeder if you are away for longer than 24 hours; the food may become stale.
- If you have more than one cat, give each one its own bowl.
- Keep the feeding area clean. Place a mat or newspaper under the food and water bowls.

◁ BOWLS
Feeding bowls are made of plastic or ceramic. The heavier the bowl, the less likely it is to be knocked over.

PLASTIC BOWL

SHORT TRIPS AWAY ▽
If a friend is unable to feed your cat, use an automatic feeder.

CAN OPENER

FORK   SPOON   KNIFE   DOUBLE BOWL

CERAMIC BOWL

△ UTENSILS
Buy a can opener, fork, knife, and spoon for cat food.

STORAGE ▷
Place plastic lids on half-full cat food cans to keep the food fresh. Store your cat's feeding kit in a plastic box.

PLASTIC LIDS   PLASTIC BOX

AUTOMATIC FEEDER

36 WHERE TO FEED

Give your cat an eating area in a quiet spot – a kitchen corner is ideal. Keep the area clean, and if you have any other pets, try to stop them from eating out of the same bowl – a larger cat, for example, may deter a kitten from feeding.

CONTENTED
EATER

37 DON'T OVERFEED

An overfed cat may become obese. This can strain its heart. If your cat is gaining weight and you are not overfeeding it, check that it is not being fed elsewhere. Excessive weight gain can also be associated with hormonal imbalance.

OVERWEIGHT
AND UNFIT

38 DAILY FEEDING NEEDS

Cats require a carefully balanced diet. As carnivores, they must eat meat regularly. The chart below is a guide to the amounts of the different types of food that you should feed your cat from the end of weaning to old age. Usually an old cat will need less food, but if it is not able to absorb its diet efficiently, it may, in fact, require more food. You should seek veterinary advice on an older cat's food intake.

Life stage	Type of complete food	Amount	Meals
2–4 months	Kitten food	3½–7 oz (100–200 g)	4–6
4–5 months	Kitten food	5–9 oz (140–250 g)	3–4
5–6 months	Kitten food	6–9 oz (170–250 g)	2–3
6–12 months	Kitten food	6–9 oz (170–250 g)	1–2
Adulthood	Canned food	5–10 oz (140–280 g)	1–2
	Semimoist food	3½–7 oz (100–200 g)	1–2
	Dry food	3½–7 oz (100–200 g)	1–2
Late pregnancy	Canned or dry food	A third more than usual	2–4
Lactation	Canned or dry food	Three times more than usual	2–4
Old age	Canned or dry food	Less food for inactive cat	1–2

39 WHY CANNED FOOD?

If you feed your cat canned food regularly, you can be sure that it has a balanced diet. Most brands of canned cat food contain all the nutrients necessary for a cat's good health, including the recommended protein intake. To give your cat variety, occasionally supplement canned food with a snack of dry, semimoist, or fresh food.

Canned white fish without bones

Canned chicken and turkey

Canned tuna chunks

Canned lamb chunks

40 WHY DRY FOOD?

Dry and semimoist foods are palatable and economical and can be bought in a variety of flavors. Feed them to your cat as directed by the manufacturer and always provide plenty of drinking water.

▽ SEMIMOIST FOOD
These are low in fats but do not store as well as canned food. They are also relatively expensive.

LIVER

SHRIMP & TUNA

SEAFOOD & VEGETABLE

DRY FOOD △
This food comes in the form of mini-biscuits, and is good for a cat's teeth.

TURKEY & CHICKEN

41 SPECIAL TREATS

Most cats enjoy treats. These tasty morsels provide variety in a cat's diet. They come in many flavors and shapes. Chews, in particular, are good for keeping your cat's gums and teeth healthy.

DAIRY COATING

DRIED FISH

BEEF & CHICKEN

CHICKEN

MILK DROPS

LIVER

42 WHICH FRESH FOODS?

Your cat will enjoy an occasional meal of fresh food, perhaps once or twice a week. However, if you feed your cat solely on fresh food, you will need to work out a nutritionally balanced diet.

◁ EGGS
Some cats like eating eggs. Try scrambling one for a light meal. Never give a cat raw egg.

△ VARIETY
A varied diet is good for a cat. Rather than sticking to one food, encourage your cat to try out any new foods that are suitable for cats.

MEAT
Bake, broil, or boil meat, and serve it slightly cooled, in small chunks or minced.

POULTRY
Most cats relish a meal of chicken, but remember to remove the bones before serving it.

FISH
Canned tuna makes a quick meal, or try steaming or poaching (but not boiling) white fish.

OATMEAL
Surprisingly, kittens enjoy oatmeal made with warm milk. Do not add sugar.

43 WHY WATER?

Although a cat obtains most of the water it needs from its food, put fresh water down at all times. A cat's water requirement depends on the amount of water present in its food and environmental conditions. Always provide fresh water when you feed your cat dried food.

44 WHY MILK?

Do not give milk to your cat as a substitute for water. It is not essential to a cat's diet, and some cats are unable to digest the lactose in cow's milk. Do not feed cow's milk to a cat with an upset stomach because it may aggravate the condition. Always serve milk fresh.

GOOD GROOMING GUIDE

45 CLIP THE CLAWS

If you keep your cat indoors permanently, get into the habit of clipping its claws regularly. If neglected, they can overgrow and pierce the paw pad. This can cause an infection, which may require veterinary treatment. Declawing (the surgical removal of claws) removes the cat's natural defense system and is definitely not advised.

GUILLOTINE-TYPE CLIPPERS

NAIL CLIPPERS

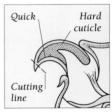

CUTTING EDGE
Do not cut to the pink quick since it causes pain and bleeding.

1 Grip the cat gently with one hand around its chest, and take hold of the paw with the other hand. Expose the claws by pressing lightly on the foot.

2 Using claw clippers or sharp nail clippers, cut off the white claw tip. If you are not sure how much to cut, be cautious and cut off just a little.

46 CLEAN THE EYES

Examine your cat's eyes regularly. Usually they will only need wiping with a cotton ball. If there is more than a small amount of clear discharge, your cat may have a disorder. Longhair cats tend to develop eye problems; their tear ducts block up and the area around the eye discolors and needs cleaning.

Check for discoloration around eye

BABY OIL

SMALL BOWL

COTTON BALLS

◁ **BE PREPARED**
Get ready for grooming by pouring a small amount of baby oil into a bowl.

△ **EYE TEST**
Before you begin cleaning your cat's eyes, examine them closely for signs of discharge.

1 After closely examining your cat's eyes, carefully wipe around each eye with a cotton ball that has been dampened in the baby oil.

2 As you wipe, try to remove any staining around the eyes. Dry the fur with a cotton ball or a tissue. Always be careful not to touch the eyeball.

47 CLEAN THE EARS

Inflammation or dark-colored wax in a cat's ear may indicate a disorder. You should only remove a foreign body if it is on the surface. If it is lodged in the canal, ask your vet to remove it.

Inspect the ear for wax

BABY OIL **SMALL BOWL** **COTTON BALLS**

◁ **BE PREPARED**
To clean your cat's ears thoroughly, you will need some baby oil, a small bowl, and a few cotton balls.

△ **EAR EXAMINATION**
When you inspect a cat's ear, do not poke anything, even a cotton swab, into it – cats' ears are very delicate.

1 After examining the ears for dark-colored wax, gently wipe away any dirt on the inside of the ear with a cotton ball, moistened in the baby oil.

2 Be very careful as you clean the ears – if you rub them too vigorously, you may damage them, or cause your cat discomfort. Use a light, circular motion.

48 CLEAN THE TEETH

Ideally, you should brush a cat's teeth once a week to prevent a buildup of scale. The earlier you accustom your cat to having its teeth brushed, the easier it will be for both of you. If your cat does not allow you to clean its teeth, ask your vet to see if your cat's teeth need descaling. This can be done under sedation.

Do not ruffle the whiskers as you open the mouth

TOOTH-PASTE   **TOOTH-BRUSH**   **COTTON SWABS**

◁ **BE PREPARED**
Do not use an ordinary toothpaste to clean your cat's teeth. You should buy a toothpaste made specifically for pets.

△ **HEALTHY TEETH & GUMS**
Cats can suffer from tooth decay and gum disease. Feeding your cat some dry food can help prevent scale deposits and gum disease.

1 Put a little toothpaste on your cat's lips to accustom it to the taste. Lightly touch the gums with a cotton swab to prepare it for the feel of a toothbrush.

2 When your cat is ready, try brushing its teeth with a toothbrush and pet toothpaste or a salt-water solution. You may need help to keep the cat still.

49 HOW TO BRUSH A SHORTHAIR

Groom your cat's coat once a week to keep it smooth and glossy. Try to groom it at the same time of day each week.

CHAMOIS CLOTH

METAL COMB

BRISTLE BRUSH

RUBBER BRUSH

◁ **BE PREPARED**
A variety of tools is required for grooming.

△ **IN THE MOOD**
Groom your cat when it is feeling relaxed.

1 Remove tangles with a metal comb, and check for the black specks that indicate flea infestation.

2 Using a bristle brush, work along the lie of the coat. Brush all the coat, including the abdomen.

3 After brushing, work through the coat with a rubber brush to smooth it and to remove dead hair.

4 Every few weeks, apply a few drops of coat conditioner. This will help to remove grease and to bring out the natural shine and color of a cat's coat.

5 Rub in the conditioner with a chamois cloth. In addition to grooming, regular stroking and a healthy diet will keep the coat looking good.

50 HOW TO BRUSH A LONGHAIR

Groom your longhair every day. As well as the obvious benefits of keeping the coat glossy and tangle-free, grooming removes loose hairs and dead skin and is beneficial to the circulation.

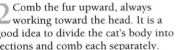

COMB   TALCUM POWDER   BRISTLE BRUSH

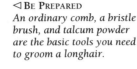

◁ BE PREPARED
An ordinary comb, a bristle brush, and talcum powder are the basic tools you need to groom a longhair.

1 Comb the fur on the abdomen and legs. Tease out knots by hand.

2 Comb the fur upward, always working toward the head. It is a good idea to divide the cat's body into sections and comb each separately.

3 If your cat is dirty, sprinkle talcum powder on its coat once a week. The talcum powder will also help you ease out any remaining tangles by hand.

4 Gently comb the fur around the neck in an upward direction, so that it forms a neck ruff.

5 Once you have combed out all the tangles, brush the coat from head to toe with a bristle brush.

6 Finish the session by brushing the tail. Gently part and brush the fur on either side.

51 GROOM A KITTEN

Although a kitten will groom itself regularly, you should help it care for its coat and teeth. The earlier you begin to groom your kitten, the sooner it will become accustomed to the procedure and the easier it will be. Always bear in mind that a kitten is both more frisky and more delicate than an adult.

SOOTHING
Before you begin, stroke the kitten.

1 Being very careful not to hurt the kitten, gently comb the coat from head to tail, easing out any tangles. Look for fleas as your comb (see p.52).

2 Once all the tangles are out, remove the dead hair by gently brushing the coat with a bristle brush. Pay attention to the legs and the area between the toes.

3 Finish by brushing your kitten's teeth and gums. It may not like this, but, if you persist, in time you should be able to brush them without difficulty.

Soft, glossy head fur

Tangle-free abdominal fur

Silky tail fur

Clean paws

52 BATHE A CAT

There may be occasions when you need to bathe your cat: its coat may be contaminated, or you may be entering it in a cat show. Most cats dislike being bathed, so you may need a helping pair of hands to soothe it. After bathing your cat, dry it quickly using a large, warm towel or try using a hair dryer.

SOFT CLOTH   CAT SHAMPOO   PLASTIC JUG

BE PREPARED △
Have the above equipment ready before you begin.

TOWEL

1 Fill a plastic bowl with warm water 4 in (10 cm) deep. Test the water temperature. Since the cat may struggle, hold it firmly as you put it into the bath.

2 Mix a little cat shampoo with warm water and, using a jug, pour it over the cat, from the neck downward. Massage the shampoo into the coat.

3 Rinse the cat with plenty of warm water, and then wrap it in a large towel and dry it off.

THE FINISHED CAT
Dry the coat with a hair dryer, unless it frightens your cat.

Clean coat is ready for grooming

UNDERSTANDING YOUR CAT

53 THE HUNTING INSTINCT

Cats are natural hunters; however much you scold a cat for hunting, you will never be able to eradicate this instinctive behavior. Do not make the mistake of assuming that your cat is hungry and is hunting for food: domestic cats will hunt even if they are fed regularly. Their prey, which they often play with, is usually small rodents or birds.

IN TRAINING
Kittens train as hunters through their play. If you give a kitten a toy, it will stalk the toy and then pounce on it.

54 A HUNTER'S GIFT

Your cat may come home with a bird or mouse in its mouth, which it proudly drops at your feet. This is meant as a contribution to the family larder, and the best thing you can do is to accept it. You should then dispose of the dead rodent or bird promptly because it may harbor disease. If you scold your cat for bringing you a gift, it will think that you are not satisfied with its offering and may hunt again in an attempt to please you.

THE HUNTER'S TROPHY
After a successful hunting trip, a cat may bring its prey into the house.

55 HELP FOR INJURED BIRDS

A distressing problem faced by cat-owners is how to help injured birds brought into the home. If you rescue an injured bird, place it in a safe, ventilated box, and take it to an animal welfare society. Do not handle the bird unless it is absolutely necessary: it will already be traumatized, and you may make it worse. Most injured birds die of shock.

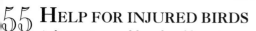

Leave nursing a bird to the experts

56 TERRITORIAL MARKING INDOORS

A cat has its own territory, which it delineates by rubbing special scent glands and spraying its urine against the points that mark the boundaries. Usually, a cat marks only its territorial boundaries outdoors. If it starts to do so indoors, it could be that it has been upset by a change in the household routine; a new cat in the home could spark this type of behavior.

△ INDOOR SPRAYING
As this can be due to ill health, and not to stress. Ask your vet to examine your cat.

SOLUTIONS ▷
Use a suitable disinfectant or cleaning solution to completely remove the odor.

57 HOW TO DEAL WITH A TIMID CAT

A timid cat holds its tail down between its legs and usually has a wary look in its eyes. It will also probably run away and hide when confronted with a stranger. Cats are not usually timid and if your cat suddenly demonstrates any of these signs, it could be due to a sudden change in its routine. If a kitten is timid, it may be that it has never become accustomed to people.

◁ **REASSURING TOUCH**
Slowly accustom the cat to being touched. Stroke and speak to it softly. Reward it with a little food.

△ **REFUGE**
A sheltered area, such as a covered bed, helps a timid cat to feel secure and gives it a refuge when it is scared.

58 THE OVERDEPENDENT CAT

An overdependent cat will follow you around, constantly seeking your attention by crying. Certain breeds, such as Siamese, seem, in general, to be more dependent. If you are away from home a lot, it is probably best not to buy a Siamese. Keep a dependent cat occupied by giving it toys or by letting it go outdoors.

◁ **ATTENTION SEEKER**
Certain signs, such as constantly alert ears, indicate a dependent cat.

△ **COMPANIONSHIP**
Give your cat a feline playmate to deflect its attention away from you.

59 STOP THAT AGGRESSION

Generally, cats do not behave aggressively toward people. If your cat suddenly tries to bite and scratch you, it may mean that it is unwell and is in pain, or that you may be handling it roughly and hurting it. Bored cats, which are kept inside permanently and not given enough toys or attention, may also become aggressive.

PLAY BITES
Your cat may bite when you play with it. These bites do not usually hurt. Be careful though if your cat is lying on its back; in this position it may feel vulnerable and become aggressive.

◁ **SUDDEN AGGRESSION**
A cat that suddenly becomes aggressive, hissing and pulling back its ears, could be unwell.

60 STOP THAT STRAYING

Usually, it is unneutered male cats and cats that are not properly cared for that stray. Cats can survive without human care and may revert to a semiferal state. Break the straying habit by calling your cat regularly at feeding times and confining it indoors for a short period.

THE NEED FOR FOOD
Feed your cat regularly to deter it from straying away from home. If you neglect your cat's appetite, it may go off in search of a new food source, probably a sympathetic neighbor.

Alert ears

Tail held high

Confident stride

61 FIGHTING SPIRIT

Unneutered male cats are usually highly territorial. They will fight with cats that trespass into their territory and for a female mate. Neutered males and females also occasionally get into cat fights, but far less often than tomcats. Neutering calms a male down.

Teeth bared

Teeth not bared

Sleek back fur

PLAY FIGHTS ▷
Play fights are important to kitten development and don't usually result in injuries. In play, a cat doesn't hiss.

△ REAL FIGHTS
In real fights, tails are puffed out and backs are arched. Serious bites occur.

62 NERVOUS GROOMING

Regular self-grooming is a natural feline occupation, but continual grooming is often a sign that a cat is anxious. Usually, nervous grooming is confined to one particular area that the cat will repeatedly chew and lick. Eventually this may lead to a skin condition or a bald patch. You should try to reassure a nervous cat, especially if a change in your routine is the cause of its behavior. If the cat does not respond to your reassurances, consult a vet, who may prescribe tranquillizers or refer you to an animal behaviorist.

A nervous cat may lick one area continually

63 THE HOUSEPLANT EATER

Your cat can be the enemy of your houseplants. It may chew the leaves and flowers and dig up the soil to use the pot as a toilet. There are two effective remedies: give your cat a pot of grass to chew (*see p.25*) or spray your plants with diluted lemon juice, which is much disliked by cats. Stop your cat digging up potted plants by placing gravel or wire mesh over the soil.

THE CURE ▽
To stop your cat from chewing the houseplants, regularly spray the foliage with diluted lemon juice; most cats dislike its taste.

THE PROBLEM ▽
A cat that is kept indoors and has no access to greenery may try to chew your houseplants.

Leaves attractive to cat

64 IMPOSING DISCIPLINE

Ensure your cat is well behaved by disciplining it as a kitten: if discipline is left until adulthood, the cat will be set in its ways. You should never try to discipline your cat using pain. A humane and effective method of discipline is to spray your cat with water from a water pistol. A very gentle tap on the nose should be given only as a last resort.

GENTLE TAP ▷
If all else fails, try a very gentle tap on the nose.

HEALTH CHECK

65 HOME MEDICAL

Unusual behavior, such as loss of appetite or lethargy, may indicate that a cat is unwell. Any persistent physical signs of ill health should be investigated by a vet – a cat may show few signs of illness before its condition is serious. You can prevent an illness from growing unchecked by regular examinations. Pick a time when your cat is feeling relaxed.

COAT
Look for scratches, fleas, baldness, discoloration of the skin, and increased shedding of hair.

EARS
Look for brown waxy discharge, swelling, and head held to one side.

Check base of tail for abscesses

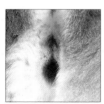

REAR END
Look for straining to pass urine, persistent licking of the genitals, and diarrhea.

HEALTHY CAT ▷
A shiny coat, vitality, ease of movement, and enjoyment of petting all indicate that your cat is well.

Lameness, swelling, or abnormal gait need investigation

ES
*ok for discharge,
lammation of the
elid, and third eye.*

TEETH
*Look for drooling,
inflamed gums, and
bad breath.*

66 SEE THE VET

It is impractical to take your cat to the vet every time you think it seems a little "off-color," but professional veterinary attention is a must if you suspect your cat has been injured, is in shock, or appears to have any persistent complaint. Calling the office for advice before you pay a visit may save you from an unnecessary expense. A vet will be able advise you on how to keep your cat in the best of health.

CALL FOR ADVICE BEFORE VISITING THE VET

67 CAT INSURANCE

Veterinary fees can be expensive, so paying a yearly insurance premium may save you money. Insurance policies cover most treatment, although routine vaccinations and neutering operations are not usually included. Some companies pay a lump sum if a cat is killed in an accident or lost.

NOSE
*Look for discharge.
Listen for labored
breathing and
persistent sneezing.*

68 FLEA SYMPTOMS

External parasites such as fleas, lice, and ticks are common on cats. The first sign of an infestation is persistent scratching. Symptoms can include visible irritation of the skin and hair loss. Fleas are visible as tiny red-brown specks, and flea droppings as small black particles. Some cats are allergic to flea droppings or saliva.

◁ THE FLEA
Pinhead-size fleas are usually found in the neck area and at the base of the tail.

△ SPRAYING
As fleas can survive off the cat's body, treat the environment as well.

1 Holding the cat still, sprinkle a suitable insecticide onto the coat.

2 Gently stroke the powder into the coat, working against the grain.

3 Once the powder has been worked through, comb out any excess.

69 USING A FLEA COLLAR

If your cat has had a flea infestation and you have taken all the appropriate measures, including disinfecting bedding and furnishings, putting a flea collar on your cat will prevent further infestation. A flea collar provides continuous antiflea medication. If, at any time, the cat shows visible signs of irritation around the neck, remove the collar.

Regularly remove the collar to check for irritation

70 TESTING THE EYES

Discharge, closure, or any cloudiness of the eye are all signs of an eye problem, as is the appearance of the third eyelid (*see below*). Most eye conditions can be treated with the appropriate eye drops. If a serious eye condition is not treated, it may result in blindness. A cat that loses its sight usually compensates for the loss by developing its other senses, and so manages to cope well. If you suspect there is something wrong with your cat's eyes, ask your vet for advice.

◁ **EYE TREATMENT**
Never put drops or ointment into a cat's eye without consulting the vet. Your vet will examine the eyes closely using an ophthalmoscope to look into the deeper parts of the eyes.

△ **TEST A CAT'S EYESIGHT**
Cover one eye and move a finger slowly toward the other eye. If the cat blinks, its eyesight is probably fine.

71 THE THIRD EYELID

Cats have an extra eyelid – called the third eyelid – to protect their eyes. This eyelid is a nictitating membrane situated at the inner corner of each eye. It is persistently visible only when the cat is ill or hurt – it may have lost weight, be suffering from diarrhea or cat influenza, or have damaged an eye in a fight. If only one eye is showing its third eyelid, it is probably due to the eye itself being damaged rather than to the cat being unwell. If your cat's third eyelid is visible, take it to the vet for an examination.

VISIBLE THIRD EYELID

72 HOW TO TREAT EAR MITES

Ear mites are not usually a problem unless they are present in large numbers. They feed on the lining of the ear canal, causing the production of a brown wax. Signs that your cat has a problem with ear mites are persistent scratching of the ears and head shaking. If the infection spreads to the inner ear, the cat's hearing and balance may be affected.

THE EAR MITE
These tiny mites can be clearly seen with an auriscope. If mites are present, your vet will usually prescribe drops.

ITCHY EARS
Persistent scratching is a sure sign that your cat has something wrong with its ears.

73 EAR INJURIES

A cat's ears are vulnerable to all types of injury. Cat fights can leave them torn and infected. Persistent scratching can cause a blood blister; left untreated, this may lead to a deformed ear. The ears of white cats are prone to frostbite (*see p.69*) and sunburn, which can lead to cancer. Ask your vet about suitable barrier creams to prevent growths.

◁ **TREATMENT**
If you think your cat has an ear disorder, ask your vet to examine it. Ear drops are a common medication for ear disorders and are easily administered (see p.62).

△ **EAR EXAMINATION**
A vet will examine your cat's ears with an auriscope – an instrument that enables the lower part of the ear canal to be viewed. Never push anything in the ear – cats' delicate ears can be damaged easily.

74 WORMS

Many cats are prone to harboring internal parasites such as the lungworm, which lives in the lungs and causes respiratory problems. Blood-sucking hookworms live in the small intestine, and can cause anemia. Common cat-infesting parasites are the roundworm and tapeworm that live in the intestines.

◁ LUNGWORM CYCLE
A cat will be infected by lungworm if it eats a bird or rodent that has eaten a snail or slug that fed on lungworm larvae.

△ THE LISTENING VET
A persistent dry cough can indicate the presence of lungworms. By listening to the cat's breathing, the vet can check for infection.

75 HOW TO WORM YOUR CAT

The symptoms of internal parasites vary but usually include diarrhea, anemia, and loss of weight. Affected kittens can be severely weakened and should be given worming tablets from about four weeks old. Adult cats should be checked twice a year. The tablets prescribed vary according to the type of worm infestation.

WORMING
The medicine comes in a paste that you add to food, or in tablet form.

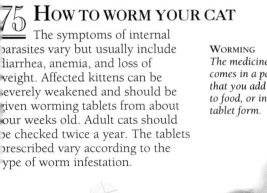

ROUNDWORM
TABLETS

TAPEWORM
TABLETS

76 DIARRHEA

Diarrhea in a cat can be caused by a variety of disorders. It could be a sign of an illness such as Feline Infectious Enteritis, or the result of a food allergy or intolerance. If the diarrhea is persistent, you should take your cat to the vet. If severe diarrhea is allowed to continue unchecked, the cat could die through dehydration.

VET CHECKS FOR SWOLLEN ABDOMEN

77 WHAT CAUSES VOMITING?

Cats do occasionally vomit. This may occur because the cat is protecting itself from a harmful substance that it has swallowed, or it may be getting rid of hairballs. However, if vomiting is prolonged, if it is accompanied by diarrhea, or if blood is present, it may be a sign of a serious illness. If a cat is also suffering from abdominal pain and excessive thirst, it may have been poisoned. In any case, if vomiting is persistent or continuous, consult your vet without delay.

78 WHAT CAUSES APPETITE LOSS?

Although an illness can lead to appetite loss, it can also be caused by something as simple as hot weather. Never force food into a cat's mouth. Tempt it with new foods, or warm small amounts of a favorite food to blood temperature several times a day. However, if your cat refuses all food for more than 24 hours, consult a vet. Take away any uneaten food after ten minutes or so.

NO APPETITE
If your cat refuses to eat consider whether the food is fresh before worrying about illness

79 HOW TO TREAT INFLUENZA

The term "cat flu" covers several types of respiratory virus. Prevention of some of these is possible by vaccination, although for others no vaccination is yet available. Treatment is usually by a course of antibiotics followed by careful home nursing. Sneezing, coughing, and runny eyes and nose are all common flu symptoms. Cat flu can be serious and can spread quickly. Prompt veterinary treatment is therefore essential.

KEEP A SICK CAT WARM

80 PREVENT GUM DISEASE

Although it is uncommon for a cat to suffer from tooth decay, gum disease, which can lead to loss of teeth, can occur. To prevent serious gum disease, regularly check your cat's mouth for signs of a disorder. Dental problems are usually due to a buildup of scale on the teeth. This can lead to gum inflammation, known as gingivitis, or an infection of the tooth socket, which can lead to an abscess forming.

Regularly examine your cat's mouth

◁ **GINGIVITIS**
The first sign of gingivitis appears as a dark red line along the gum. The gums will recede and teeth may be lost. Contact your vet if you suspect gingivitis.

△ **CLEAN THE TEETH**
Most dental problems can be avoided if you clean your cat's teeth (see p.39). Feeding your cat dry food will help remove debris from the teeth.

81 RECOGNIZING URINARY PROBLEMS

Cat's urine should be clear or pale yellow and passed easily. If a cat strains or if the urine is cloudy or discolored, it may be ill. Most feline urinary problems are caused by bladder infections, kidney diseases, or diabetes. A blockage of the bladder, known as Feline Urological Syndrome, causes the cat to strain and pass bloodstained urine; it is painful and requires urgent veterinary attention.

STRAINING
Urinary disorders can be painful and distressing to a cat.

82 KIDNEY DISEASE SYMPTOMS

Kidney disease can be chronic or acute. Chronic kidney disease is common in older cats. Its symptoms include increased thirst, frequent urination, weight loss, bad breath, and mouth ulcers. Younger cats tend to suffer from acute kidney disease. It is usually caused by an infection, and its symptoms include vomiting and dehydration. Both types require veterinary attention.

OLDER CATS
As a cat grows old, its kidneys may deteriorate. A careful diet and medical treatment are needed if the cat is to survive.

◁ **THIRSTY CAT**
An excessive thirst and frequent urination are common symptoms of kidney disease.

83 WHEN A CAT SCRATCHES

Cats are not usually aggressive toward humans but may scratch and bite in play. Cat scratches can easily become infected in humans. If a cat scratch becomes infected, consult your doctor. As a preventative measure, clean the wound with antiseptic.

◁ **BITES**
Rabies is carried in the saliva of certain animals. If you are bitten by a cat in a country where rabies is present, seek immediate medical attention.

SCRATCHES ▷
A fever following a cat scratch may indicate cat-scratch fever.

84 HUMAN HEALTH DANGERS

The most serious cat-related health hazard for humans is rabies. Other transferable diseases are Toxoplasmosis, caused by a parasite that can be present in cat droppings, and various skin infections such as ringworm. These diseases are not serious, although pregnant women can be at risk from Toxoplasmosis.

Sensible hygiene leads to safety

Keep to sensible hygiene rules to prevent infection. Handle soiled cat litter carefully, and, if your cat has an infection, disinfect bedding and grooming equipment. The risk of infection from your cat is then minimal.

NURSING A CAT

85 HOW TO ADMINISTER MEDICINE

When it comes to swallowing medicine, cats, like children, can be troublesome. A helping hand will make life much easier, especially when it comes to holding the cat still. Be firm but not rough. Hiding medicine in food doesn't usually work – cats are good at detecting it.

1 Ask an assistant to hold the cat still while you grip it firmly around the head. Take care not to ruffle its whiskers.

2 Holding the head with forefinger and thumb, tip it back. With the other hand, lightly press on the jaw to open the mouth.

3 Place the tablet on the back of the tongue. Close the mouth and stroke the throat. Check that the tablet goes down.

DOSING WITH A SYRINGE
Administer liquid medicine with a syringe. Slowly squirt into the side of the mouth.

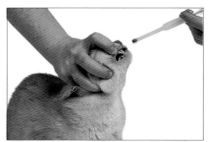

DOSING WITH A DOSING GUN
A dosing gun enables you to give a tablet by "firing" it into the back of the throat.

86 HOW TO APPLY EYE OINTMENT

You should never apply ointment to a cat's eyes unless it has been prescribed by a vet. Administer the ointment quickly by squeezing about ¼–½ in (5–10 mm) directly onto the eye, using a minimum amount of force. You will need to hold the cat firmly to keep it still as you do this.

1 Hold the cat's head firmly with one hand, and squeeze the ointment onto the eyeball.

2 Close the eyelids for a few seconds, enabling the ointment to spread evenly over the eye.

87 HOW TO APPLY EYE DROPS

Eye drops are commonly prescribed for various eye disorders. Before applying them, you need to clean around the cat's eyes to clear any discharge. Use a cotton ball dampened in clean, warm water. If there is any soreness, apply a little petroleum jelly, but do not put it too close to the cat's eyes. You should never give a cat eye drops unless they have been prescribed by the vet, nor give more drops in one session than you have been advised to do by your vet.

1 Take hold of the cat's head firmly, and wipe away any discharge.

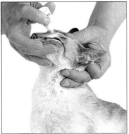

2 Carefully squeeze the prescribed number of drops into each eye.

3 Close the eyes for a moment to allow them to bathe in the drops.

88 HOW TO APPLY EAR DROPS

If you notice any discharge in your cat's ears, persistent scratching or rubbing of the ears, a swelling of the ear flaps, or side-to-side head shaking, consult a vet. Ear drops are a commonly prescribed medication for ear disorders. It is important to know how to apply them correctly.

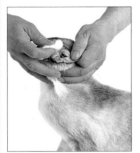

1 Carefully wipe away any visible dirt or discharge from the inside of the ear flap with a moistened cotton ball.

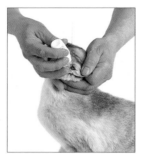

2 Hold the head, and gently fold the outer ear back, so that the ear flap is exposed. Apply the correct number of drops.

3 Once you have applied the drops, very gently massage them into the ear. Be careful not to poke the dropper into the ears.

89 KEEPING A SICK CAT WARM

A cat that is unwell or is recovering from an operation needs careful nursing. It should be placed in a quiet and clean area, away from the hubbub of the household. A cardboard box makes a good sick bed. Ensure that it is comfortable and warm. Cut away about two-thirds of one side of the box and line it with newspaper and a blanket, and, if necessary, add a lukewarm hot-water bottle. For extra warmth, wrap a large towel around the cat.

CARE BOX
A cardboard box, lined with newspaper and a blanket, makes a good sick bed for a cat.

90 SICK CAT MEALS

A sick cat may be prescribed a special diet by the vet, which it does not like, or it may go off its usual food. Loss of appetite can be very worrying for a cat owner, but some gentle coaxing will usually encourage a cat to eat. Try feeding your cat small meals, warmed to blood temperature, several times a day. If your cat is very weak and still will not eat, try syringe feeding, although this should be a last resort.

SPOON-FEEDING LIQUID
If your cat refuses liquids and solids, try spoon-feeding some liquid. Grip the head and spoon-feed a few drops at a time.

SPOON-FEEDING MEDICINE
To spoon-feed a cat liquid medicine, grip the head between forefinger and thumb and feed the cat, giving it time to swallow.

SYRINGE FEEDING
If a cat is very weak, it may have to be fed with a syringe. Liquefy the food and feed it to the cat with a dropper or syringe.

91 CARE FOR ELDERLY CATS

An old cat will usually sleep more and eat less than a young cat. Around ten years, a cat's condition begins to deteriorate; its hearing may weaken, its coat may become thinner, and its joints and muscles may stiffen. Keep a careful check on your cat's condition. In particular, look for signs of kidney disease; symptoms include excessive thirst and urination. If your cat becomes ill or is in pain and the condition is untreatable, you can ask the vet to "put it to sleep." The vet will give the cat an injection of anesthetic, which will end its life peacefully.

FIRST AID

92 TREAT AN UNCONSCIOUS CAT

Cats do have accidents: they may be hit by a car or fall from a considerable height and be knocked unconscious or into a state of shock. If you find an injured cat, try to assess its injuries and, if you are able, administer first aid, either to make it more comfortable or to save its life. If the cat is in shock – it will feel cold and have a rapid pulse – keep it warm by wrapping it in a blanket. Take the cat to the vet as soon as possible. All first aid is an interim to veterinary attention.

1 If you find an unconscious cat, your first priority should be to move it out of harm's way and take it to a vet. Using a blanket as a stretcher, lay it out flat and gently lift the cat onto it.

2 With the help of another person, carefully lift the blanket up and place it on a flat, steady surface. If the cat is having difficulty breathing, turn it onto its side with its head tilted downward, and open its mouth, pulling the tongue forward. Gently clean the mouth of mucus with a cotton swab.

3 Don't let the cat lie on one side for more than five to ten minutes or give it anything by mouth. To take the cat to the vet, lower the blanket into a secure container, such as a cardboard box.

93 HOW TO LIFT AN INJURED CAT

If you attempt to help a cat with a suspected broken limb, you must handle it very carefully. Do not apply a splint yourself since this may distress the cat further. Pick the cat up and place it on a blanket, keeping the broken limb uppermost. Try to prevent the limb from being moved in any way. Place the cat in a cat carrier, and take it to the vet.

INJURED CAT CARRIED ON BLANKET

94 HOW TO STOP BLEEDING

If a cat is cut and bleeding and the wound is not too deep, you can probably treat it yourself. Clean the wound with a damp cotton ball, cut away any matted fur, and apply a mild antiseptic. Petroleum jelly applied to the edges of the wound prevents hair from falling into it. If your cat is bleeding heavily, take the following steps to stop the flow. If the bleeding doesn't stop, take the cat to the vet as soon as possible.

1 To stop the bleeding, cover the wound with a gauze pad soaked in cold water (known as a cold-water compress) and apply pressure.

2 If the bleeding doesn't stop, secure the gauze with a bandage and put a gauze pad over the top.

3 To secure the dressing, wrap another bandage around the gauze pad and apply pressure. If the bleeding was heavy, take the cat to the vet.

95 FIGHT WOUNDS

A cat that is allowed outside may come home with scratches and cuts that it has received in fights with other cats. It may look disheveled, have patches of fur missing, and have scratches on its eyelids and ears. Usually, these wounds are only superficial and do not require veterinary attention. You can clean minor scratches, for example, with a mild antiseptic. If a wound gets infected, treat it yourself (*see p.68*) or, if an abscess develops, take the cat to a vet. Heavy bleeding should be treated immediately (*see p.65*).

Ears are vulnerable to bites

Examine eyelids for cuts

Check for abscesses at base of tail

96 ACTION FOR POISON

If a cat swallows a poisonous substance, it will usually vomit. Occasionally, however, the cat will actually digest the poison. Act promptly if your cat shows signs of poisoning (*see p.67*). If a cat's coat is contaminated, it may attempt to lick off the poison, only to ingest it. Wash off the poison with diluted shampoo. If this does not work, take the cat and a sample of the poison to the vet. Do not induce vomiting.

Drooling from mouth

REACTION
If your cat has been poisoned, it will probably collapse. Contact the vet, who will need to know the type of poison swallowed by the cat.

Collapsed body

Spilled substance

97 POISON KNOW-HOW

This chart indicates some common substances that are toxic to a cat. If your cat swallows any of these, veterinary treatment is essential. Some substances, such as painkillers, can be fatal to a cat.

Poison	Signs of Poisoning	Action
Rodent poisons	Restlessness, abdominal pain, vomiting, bleeding, and diarrhea. Potentially fatal.	Consult vet Antidotes available
Antifreeze	Lack of coordination, vomiting, convulsions followed by coma.	Injection may block the effect
Alcohol	Depression, vomiting, collapse, dehydration, and coma.	Potentially fatal Consult vet
Painkillers	Loss of balance, vomiting. Gums may turn blue if swallowed.	Potentially fatal Consult vet
Disinfectants & cleaners	Severe vomiting, diarrhea, nervous signs, staggering, and coma.	Potentially fatal Consult vet
Insecticides & pesticides	Muscle twitching, drooling, convulsions, and coma.	Consult vet No specific antidote
Slug & snail poisons	Salivation, muscle twitching, vomiting, diarrhea, convulsions, and coma.	Veterinary treatment effective if prompt

Poisonous Plants

- Azalea
- Caladium
- Christmas Rose
- Clematis
- Delphinium
- Dieffenbachia
- Ivy
- Lupine
- Mistletoe
- Oleander
- Philodendron
- Poinsettia
- Cherry Laurel
- Rhododendron
- Solanum
- Sweet Pea

SWEET PEA

POINSETTIA

CLEMATIS

SOLANUM

LUPINE

98 TREATING A STING

A cat stung by a bee or wasp may suffer discomfort; the stung area will swell and the cat may appear unsteady and short of breath. Look closely for a red, swollen area that resembles a splinter wound. If it is a bee sting, try to remove it with tweezers. If you are unsuccessful, seek veterinary advice.

Remove bee sting with tweezers

99 ABSCESS AID

If a cat has been bitten by another cat and the wound doesn't heal, an abscess may develop. The wound will get infected and, after a few days, swell. If the abscess is especially large, and you are unable to treat it, ask your vet to lance it.

1 ▷ Very gently, clip away the fur surrounding the swollen area. Ask a friend to reassure the cat as you clip.

2 To bring the abscess to a head, bathe the area with a solution made up of one teaspoon of salt to a glass of water.

3 If bathed regularly for 24 hours, the abscess should burst. Clean the area, and check that the abscess doesn't return.

100 SOOTHING A SCALD

If your cat suffers a burn or scald, perhaps from an open fire or boiling water, your first priority is to take it to a vet as soon as possible. You can help to alleviate the pain by following the steps set out below. If your cat suffers an electrical burn, take it straight to the vet. Severe electrical burns can result in heart failure.

1 Swab the scald with cold water. Do not apply cream or butter to the wound.

2 Hold an ice pack (made from ice cubes held in a freezer bag or cloth) against the wound.

3 Apply petroleum jelly to the wound. Do not cover the burn or cut away the surrounding fur.

101 HELP IN COLD WEATHER

When the weather is very cold, a cat may suffer from frostbite and hypothermia. Veterinary attention is essential since the cold may send the cat into shock. The cat will be cold and stiff with what appear to be "burns" at the extremities.

FROSTBITE ▷
If a cat is suffering from frostbite, bathe the affected area in warm water. (Ears, paws, and tail are the most commonly affected areas.) Then, keeping the cat warm, take it to the vet.

△ HYPOTHERMIA
This can result in death. Wrap the cat in blankets to warm it. Call the veterinary practice for advice.

INDEX

INDEX

ACKNOWLEDGMENTS

Dorling Kindersley would like to thank Hilary Bird for compiling the index, Ann Kay for proofreading, Murdo Culver for design assistance, and Mark Bracey for computer assistance.

Photography
KEY: t *top*; b *bottom*; c *center*; l *left*; r *right*
All photographs by Steve Gorton and Tim Ridley except for:
Peter Anderson 27tr; Paul Bricknell 16cl, 18, 20tl, 22bl, 23cl, 25l, 26c, 33tl, 51cr; Jane Burton 1, 2, 5, 8tr, 8bl, 9bl, 10tr, 13cl, 14tr, 15cr, 16tc, 19bl, 20cr, 21cr, 22tr, 22cl, 23tr, 25bl, 23bl, 25tl, 25cr, 44tl, 44br, 45tr, 45br, 45 bl, 45bl, 46tl, 46tr, 46br, 47tr, 47tl, 47b, 48tl, 48cl, 48br, 49br, 52cr, 52cc, 52cl, 53cl, 54tr, 54bl, 59tl, 59tr, 59br, 71, 72; Bruce Coleman Ltd/Jane Burton 53br; Tom Dobbie 67ct, 67bl Marc Henrie 3, 6, 7, 9br, 10c, 11, 12 tr, 12cl, 13tr, 13b, 28cr, 28br, 36tc, 46bl, 50–51c; Daniel Pangbourne 22br; Colin Walton 28tl, 34b, 67c, 67bc, 67br; Matthew Ward 60.

Illustrations
Angelica Elsebach 64, 65, 66, 68, 69;
Chris Forsey 15, 16, 24, 27, 31, 52, 54, 55.